MUSIC LITERATURE

A WORKBOOK FOR ANALYSIS

VOLUME I: HOMOPHONY

GORDON HARDY AND ARNOLD FISH

JUILLIARD SCHOOL OF MUSIC

HARPER & ROW, PUBLISHERS   NEW YORK   HAGERSTOWN   SAN FRANCISCO   LONDON

UNDER THE ADVISORY EDITORSHIP OF
JACK M. WATSON
Dean, College-Conservatory of Music
of the University of Cincinnati

MUSIC LITERATURE   A Workbook for Analysis
VOLUME I: Homophony

Library of Congress Catalog Card Number: 62-19671
Standard Book Number: 06-042633-0

More and more during the past decade or so has the pedagogical purpose of music theory been defined as the development of musical understanding—understanding not only of music of the common-practice period, the eighteenth and nineteenth centuries, but rather of music of all periods. More and more, too, has the approach shifted from deduction to induction. "Students should learn about music," to personify the trend, "not by memorizing abstract rules (isolated from music literature and applicable at best only to the common-practice period) and spending endless hours on abstract exercises based on these rules, but by studying music itself and at first hand identifying characteristics that determine the style of a piece, of a composer, of a period, or of a nation." And more and more has musical style become the core of this empirical approach to musical understanding.

The purpose seemed valid, the approach reasonable, and the implied program in outline clear and pedagogically sound. But instructors have had an inordinately difficult time implementing it, simply because suitable materials have not been available. From institutions have come reports of various practices—use of collections of keyboard music, purchase by students of a sample of musical scores, requisition of multiple copies from the reference library—all, for one reason or another, unsatisfactory.

Messrs. Hardy and Fish have gone a long way toward resolving the problem with this workbook. (The second book in this workbook series centers on polyphonic music.) The authors have provided under a single cover a sample of music literature representative of most periods, styles, forms, and types of music, yet sufficiently simple for first- and second-year undergraduate music theory and analysis courses. But they have done more than provide a carefully selected collection of music materials, important as this in itself is. By means of simple and direct questions and suggestions (and a few specimen analyses) they have produced the essentials of a comprehensive yet flexible learning program—and one readily adapted to a variety of approaches and course organizations—aimed squarely at the development of musical understanding.

Through the questions and suggestions students are led to probe deeply and broadly into the structure and stylistic determinants of individual compositions. They are guided into making significant comparisons, and on the bases of these comparisons to arrive at generalizations. They are steered toward the discovery of fundamental relationships, they are stimulated to search for influences, and they are led to see the operation of over-all aesthetic principles. And within this multi-dimensional program of analysis and synthesis, musical performance is kept in sharp focus with guiding questions concerning the influence or implications of relevant factors for intelligent musical performance.

It would be difficult to conceive of any field in the entire musical profession where students preparing for a career would not benefit greatly from thoroughly "working through" this book. The music is of aesthetic worth and ideal for analytical purposes. And the instructional notes focus on bedrock so far as musical understanding is concerned. The authors have provided students (and teachers) with a practical tool that can contribute in a major way to the development of musical intelligence and discrimination.

Jack M. Watson

Bloomington, Indiana

FOREWORD

This workbook has been designed for use in first- and second-year classes in Theory, Harmony, and Form and Analysis. The examples selected represent a broad sampling of music that we have been using in our classes at Juilliard. The material is, for the most part, homophonic music from the seventeenth to the nineteenth century, but many works from other periods in music history are included to give a wide scope of musical practice.

The music (complete works or movements whenever possible) is organized in large units offering a varied musical experience. The unit on melody (Unit I) is arranged in historical groups, with those excerpts having the clearest phrasing, tonality, and structure presented first. The short piano works and chorales (Units II and III) are graded harmonically; first, diatonic pieces; then, those having simple modulations; and finally, more complex, chromatic, and contemporary examples. The songs (Unit IV) introduce the problems of text setting, vocal considerations, and the traditions of the Lied. Practical applications of figured bass are presented in Unit V. Unit VI has clear examples of Sonata-Allegro and Rondo forms. Several excerpts from orchestral works are included in Unit VII as an introduction to instruments of the orchestra, transposing instruments, and score reading. Each unit is preceded by a list of suggestions and questions for analytical procedure in class or for individual study. Specimen analyses are included in the first three units to illustrate some of the possible ways in which students may write in their observations and conclusions. There is a short Appendix which presents brief definitions and examples of terms frequently used in music analysis.

The lists of suggestions and questions presented should *not* be approached in a rigid fashion. No specific order is prescribed or necessarily desirable. The creative teacher and student will, of course, approach the works in a variety of ways. The study of melody is continued throughout the entire collection. Compositional devices, modulatory techniques, comparative stylistic studies, etc. may become special areas of concentration. A general survey of phrase structure may be a focal point of study. Some of the works may be used as models for short compositions.

Constant and continuing reference by the teacher and student to those elements most directly related to performing and listening is recommended.

G. H.
A. F.

October 1, 1962

CONTENTS

UNIT I. MELODY

UNIT II. SHORT WORKS FOR PIANO

UNIT III. CHORALES

UNIT IV. SONGS

UNIT V. EXAMPLES OF FIGURED BASS

UNIT VI. THE LARGER FORMS

UNIT VII. INSTRUMENTAL EXCERPTS

APPENDIX

UNIT I

MELODY

SUGGESTIONS AND QUESTIONS FOR ANALYSIS AND DISCUSSION

A. Indicate those elements which determine the key.
   1. Final tone
   2. Key signature
   3. Opening phrase
   4. Important resting tones
   5. Chord outlines

B. Point out important rhythmic features.
   1. Rhythmic structure of the phrases
   2. Repeated rhythmic figures
   3. Related rhythmic figures
   4. Points of rest
   5. Relation of rhythmic emphasis to the meter (stress on strong beats, stress on weak beats, stress off the beat, etc.)

C. Outline and discuss the shape of the melody.
   1. Melodic curves
   2. Range
   3. Steps and leaps
   4. High points
   5. Points of rest (cadences)
   6. Chord outlines
   7. Tessitura

D. Outline the phrase structure.
   1. Large phrase groups
   2. Subdivisions in the phrase
   3. Cadences
   4. Compare the phrases

E. How do chromatic tones (if any) function?
   1. Embellishing tones
   2. Color
   3. Establishing a new tonal level

F. What are the unifying features in the melody?
   1. Related motives
   2. Compositional devices
   3. Recurring phrases
   4. Rhythmic features

G. What are the elements of contrast?
   1. Use of contrasting motives
   2. Rhythmic variety
   3. Others (key, register, etc.)

H. How do the following features influence the performance of the melody?
    1. Tempo
    2. Meter
    3. Dynamics
    4. Phrase markings
    5. Form
    6. Text setting

I. After analyzing several melodies from one era, what conclusions about style can be made?
    1. Rhythmic organization
    2. Strength of tonal center
    3. Phrase balance
    4. Chromaticism
    5. Shape of the melody (see C)

J. How do melodic lines from one period in music history differ from those of another? What do they have in common?

K. Analyze melodic lines in other units in this workbook.

L. For additional study, investigate other melodies from all periods and in all styles.

A. Beethoven, *Ninth Symphony*, Op. 125, Fourth Movement

Observations:

1. Key: D major (final tone is "d," key signature of two sharps, tonic triad is outlined on the strong beats in the first phrase — see circled notes).
2. Smooth, even rhythm in *a*; increase in rhythmic activity in *b*.
3. Cadence points have a dotted note pattern: ♩. ♪♩
4. Melody is entirely diatonic.
5. *a* has a very small range (a fifth), *b* expands the range by introducing the low "a."
6. *a* moves entirely by step; *b* presents leaps which increase in size.
7. Climax occurs at the point of the largest leap and is emphasized by the syncopation (measure 12).

B. Mozart, *Piano Sonata*, K. 281, Rondo

1. Haydn, *Symphony No. 104,* First Movement

2. Mozart, *Piano Sonata,* K. 576, First Movement

3. Mozart, *Symphony No. 41,* K. 551, Third Movement

4. Mozart, *String Quartet,* K. 575, Second Movement

5. Mozart, *Piano Concerto,* K. 491, First Movement

6. Beethoven, *Fourth Symphony,* Op. 60, Third Movement

Determine the meter. Add bar lines. Compare your markings with those in the score.

7. Beethoven, *Violin Concerto,* Op. 61, Third Movement

8. Beethoven, *String Quartet,* Op. 135, Third Movement

Determine the meter. Add bar lines.

9. Schumann, *Third Symphony,* Op. 97, First Movement

10. Schumann, *Kinderscenen,* Op. 15, Träumerei

If the strongest notes were on the strongest beats, what would the meter be?
Is this the meter that Schumann used?

11. Chopin, *Piano Concerto No. 1,* Op. 11, Second Movement

12. Chopin, *Nocturne*, Op. 48, No. 1

13. Brahms, *Fourth Symphony*, Op. 98, First Movement

Notice the recurrence and development of intervallic relationships.

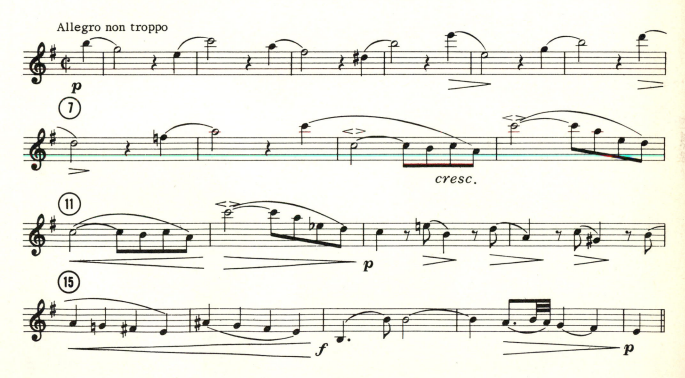

14. Brahms, *Mädchenlied*, Op. 95, No. 6

Am jüng-sten Tag ich auf-er-steh' und gleich nach mei-nem Lieb-sten seh',

und wenn ich ihn nicht fin-den kann, leg' wie-der mich zum Schla-fen

dann, leg' wie-der mich zum Schla-fen dann. O

Her-ze-leid, du E-wig-keit! Selb-an-der nur ist Se-lig-keit! Und

kommt mein Lieb-ster nicht hin-ein mag nicht im Pa-ra-die-se

sein, mag nicht im Pa-ra-die-se sein!

15. Wagner, *Tristan und Isolde*, last scene

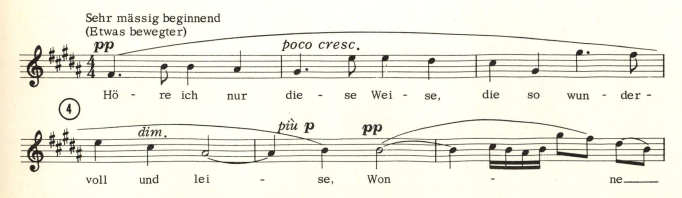

Hö-re ich nur die-se Wei-se, die so wun-der-

voll und lei-se, Won - ne

kla - gend, al - les ___ sa - gend, mild ___ ver -

söh - nend aus ___ ihm ___ tö - nend, in mich drin - get, auf sich

schwin -get, hold er - ha - lend um mich klin - get?

16. Tchaikovsky, *Fourth Symphony*, Op. 36, Second Movement

Andantino in modo di canzona

p semplice ma grazioso

17. Moussorgsky, *Pictures at an Exhibition*

18. Fauré, *Chanson d'Amour,* Op. 27, No. 1

J'ai - me tes yeux, j'ai - me ton front, O ma re - belle, ô ma fa -

rou - che, J'ai - me tes yeux, j'ai - me ta bou - che Où mes bai - sers s'é - pui - se - ront.

J'ai - me ta voix, j'ai - me l'é - tran - ge grâ - ce de tout ce que tu

dis, Ô ma re - belle, ô mon cher an - ge, mon en - fer et mon pa - ra -

dis! J'ai - me tes yeux, j'ai - me ton front, Ô ma re - bel - le, ô ma fa - rou - che,

J'ai - me tes yeux, j'ai - me ta bou - che Où mes bai - sers s'é - pui - se - ront.

19. R. Strauss, *Till Eulenspiegel,* Op. 28

MELODIES FROM THE 17th AND 18th CENTURIES

20. Corelli, *Sonata* for violin and cembalo, Op. 5, No. 8, Sarabande

21. Vivaldi, *Concerto in D Minor* for oboe, strings and cembalo, First Movement

22. Purcell, *Ode for Saint Cecilia's Day*, Aria

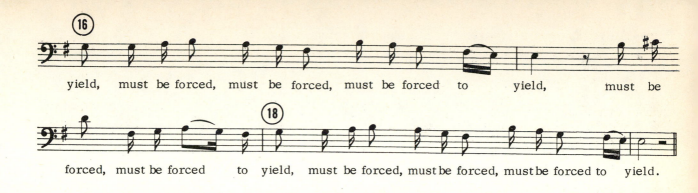

yield,   must be forced,   must be   forced,   must be forced   to   yield,   must be

forced,   must be forced   to   yield,   must be forced,   must be forced,   must be forced to   yield.

23. Rameau, *Dardanus*, Air en Rondeau

24. Handel, *Alcina*, Gavotte

25. Bach, *Brandenburg Concerto No. 2*, First Movement
  Determine the meter. Add bar lines.

26. Bach, *B Minor Mass*, Agnus Dei

A – gnus De – i, qui tol – lis pec – ca –

ta mun – di, qui tol – lis pec – ca – ta pec – ca – ta

mun – di, mi – se – re – re no – bis, mi – se – re –

re no - bis, mi - se - re - re no - bis, qui tol - lis pec -

ca - ta pec - ca - ta mun - di, mi - se - re - re no - bis.

PLAINSONGS

27.

Ky - ri - e e - le - i - son (iij)

Chri - ste e - le - i - son (iij)

Ky - ri - e e - le - i - son (ij)

Ky - ri - e e - le - i - son

17

28.

Al - le - lu - i - a   (ij)

29.

A - ve Ma - ri - - a, gra - ti - a ple - - na: Do - mi - nus

te - cum: be - ne - di - cta tu in mu - li - - e - ri - bus.

MELODIES FROM THE 14th TO 17th CENTURIES

30. Machaut, *Je puis trop bien*

Je   puis   trop   bien   ma

da - me com - par - er   a   l'y - ma - ge

que fist Py - ma - li - on.

que Me - de - e Ja - zon.

31. 15th century folk song, *L'homme armé*

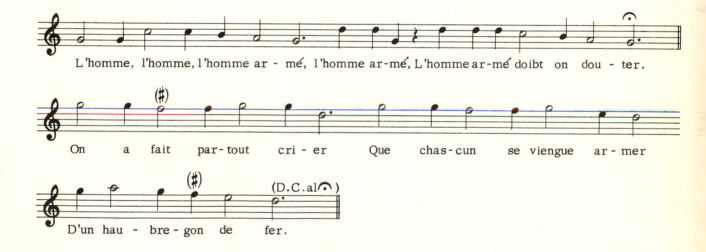

L'homme, l'homme, l'homme ar - mé, l'homme ar-mé, L'homme ar-mé doibt on dou - ter.

On a fait par-tout cri - er Que chas-cun se viengue ar - mer

D'un hau - bre-gon de fer.

32. Palestrina, *Exultate Deo*

Ex - ul - ta - te De - o, ad - ju -
to - ri nos - tro, ad ju to -
ri nos - tro.

33. Schütz, *Psalm*

Outline the broad rhythmic pattern.

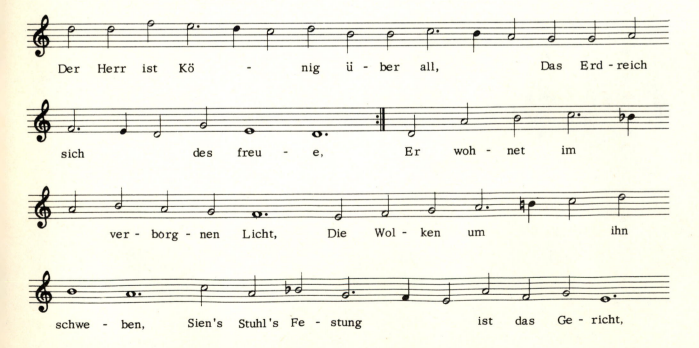

Der Herr ist Kö - nig ü - ber all, Das Erd - reich
sich des freu - e, Er woh - net im
ver - borg - nen Licht, Die Wol - ken um ihn
schwe - ben, Sien's Stuhl's Fe - stung ist das Ge - richt,

Ge - rech - tig - keit   da - ne - ben,

Da - nach die Welt   soll stre - ben.

MELODIES FROM THE 20th CENTURY

34. Debussy, *String Quartet in G Minor*, First Movement

Is there a central tonality?

35. Debussy, *Préludes*, Book 1, Voiles

36. Stravinsky, *Petrouchka*

Compare this melody with the Plainsongs.

37. Stravinsky, *Symphony of Psalms,* Second Movement

Compare this melody with the excerpt from Brahms Fourth Symphony. (No.13)

38. Schönberg, *Piano Concerto,* Op. 42, First Movement

A twelve-tone melody. How does it differ from other melodies in this unit?

39. Hindemith, *Third Piano Sonata,* Fourth Movement

40. Bartók, *Music for Strings, Percussion and Celeste*

41. Prokofieff, *Symphony No. 5,* Op. 100, Second Movement

42. Copland, *Sonata for Violin and Piano*, First Movement

43. Schuman, *Third Symphony*, Passacaglia

UNIT II

SHORT WORKS FOR PIANO

SUGGESTIONS AND QUESTIONS FOR ANALYSIS AND DISCUSSION

A. What is the basic key center of the work? How did you determine this?

B. Outline the work melodically. (See Unit I, page 1.)

C. Analyze the harmonic structure of numbers 1-23.
   1. Identify the root and quality of each chord.
   2. Using Roman numerals and figured bass symbols, indicate the harmonic function of each chord.
   3. Identify and compare the cadences.
   4. Do modulations occur? Where? Relate the new key(s) to the basic key center.
   5. Circle and name the nonharmonic tones.

D. Indicate and discuss the elements which contribute to unity and variety in the work.
   1. Phrase lengths
   2. Rhythmic features
   3. Use of figures and motives
   4. Compositional devices
   5. Accompaniment patterns
   6. Texture

E. Outline the over-all formal structure

F. Discuss other significant aspects of this work which lead to an intelligent musical performance.
   1. Rhythm and tempo
   2. High points
   3. Use of dynamics
   4. Type of composition (dance, character piece, etc.)
   5. Historical considerations

G. Compare the contemporary works (24-26) with the other pieces in this unit.
   1. Establishment of key
   2. Chord structure
   3. Cadences
   4. Other elements (texture, rhythm, etc.)

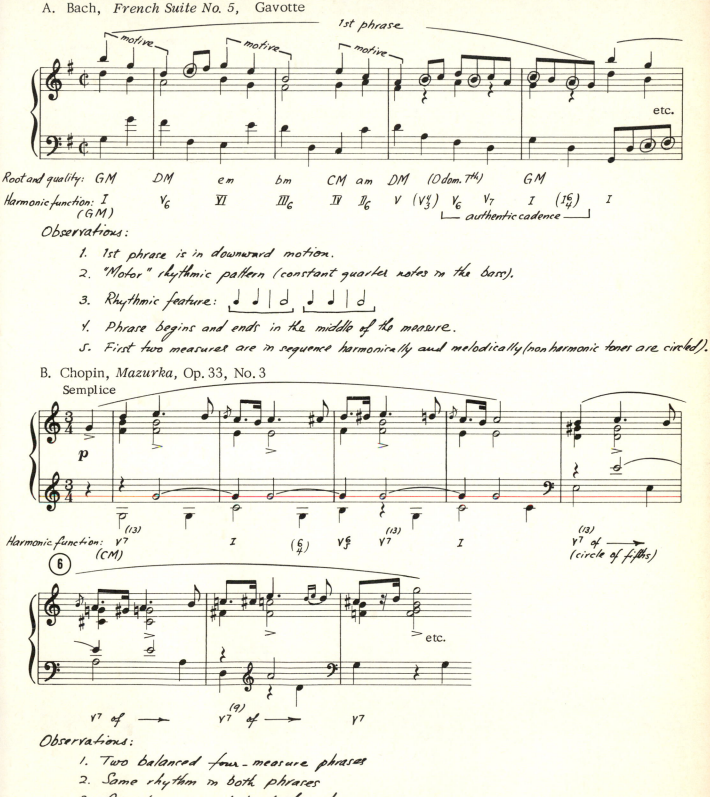

A. Bach, *French Suite No. 5*, Gavotte

Root and quality: GM   DM   em   bm   CM am   DM   (0 dom. 7th)   GM

Harmonic function: I   V₆   VI   III₆   IV II₆   V (V⁴₃)   V₆   V₇   I   (I⁶₄)   I
(GM)   authentic cadence

Observations:

1. 1st phrase is in downward motion.
2. "Motor" rhythmic pattern (constant quarter notes in the bass).
3. Rhythmic feature:
4. Phrase begins and ends in the middle of the measure.
5. First two measures are in sequence harmonically and melodically (nonharmonic tones are circled).

B. Chopin, *Mazurka*, Op. 33, No. 3

Semplice

Harmonic function: V⁷   I   (⁶₄)   V⁶₅ V⁷   I   V⁷ of →
(CM)   (circle of fifths)

⑥

V⁷ of →   V⁷ of →   V⁷

Observations:

1. Two balanced four-measure phrases
2. Same rhythm in both phrases
3. Accent on second beat of each measure
4. Constant repetition of motive

27

DANCE

Beethoven

2.

Beethoven

3.

Schubert

4.

DANCE

Schubert

GERMAN DANCE

Schubert

6.

GAVOTTE

from *French Suite No. 5*

Bach

7.

THEME AND VARIATION
from *The Carman's Whistle*

Theme

Byrd

Variation 2

8.

THEME AND VARIATION

from *Seven Variations on "God Save the King"*

Theme

Beethoven

34

Variation 1

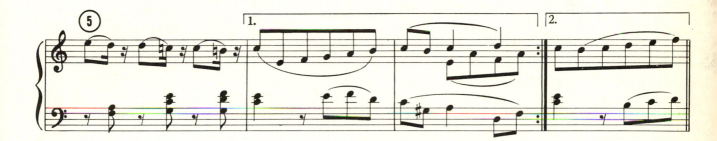

9.

THEME AND VARIATION

from Variations and Fugue on a Theme by Handel

Aria

Brahms, Op. 24

Variation 1

PRELUDE

Chopin, Op. 28, No. 3

11. VON FREMDEN LÄNDERN UND MENSCHEN

from *Kinderscenen*

Schumann, Op. 15, No. 1

12.

SARABANDE

from *French Suite No. 1*

Bach

WALTZ

from *Albumblätter*

Lebhaft

Schumann, Op. 124, No. 4

MAZURKA

Allegro ma non troppo

Chopin, Op. 68, No. 3

Poco piu vivo

Tempo I

MAZURKA

Chopin, Op. 67, No. 2

Cantabile

16.

Vivo ma non troppo

Chopin, Op. 7, No. 2

17.

KANONISCHES LIEDCHEN

from *Album für die Jugend*

Nicht schnell und mit innigem Ausdruck

Schumann, Op. 68, No. 27

SONG WITHOUT WORDS

Presto

Mendelssohn, Op. 102, No. 3

19.

SONG WITHOUT WORDS

Mendelssohn, Op. 62, No. 3

54

SONG WITHOUT WORDS

Andante espressivo

Mendelssohn, Op. 19, No. 2

21. PRELUDE

Largo

Chopin, Op. 28, No. 4

INTERMEZZO

Moderato semplice

Brahms, Op. 76, No. 7

INTERMEZZO

Grazioso e giocoso

Brahms, Op. 119, No. 3

molto **p** e leggiero

sost.   sost.

legato

un poco rit.

24.

SIXTH BAGATELLE

from *Bagatelles for Piano*

Lento ♩ = 69

Bartók, Op. 6

THE CAT

from *The Household Muse*

Milhaud

CHILDREN AT PLAY

from *Little Suite*

Harris

Copyright 1939 by G. Schirmer, Inc. Reprinted by permission.

A THREE-SCORE SET

(Second Movement)

Schuman

UNIT III

CHORALES

SUGGESTIONS AND QUESTIONS FOR ANALYSIS AND DISCUSSION

A. Examine the melodic structure.
   1. Sing the chorale melody. Analyze its shape and rhythmic structure. Point out any phrases that are related by means of repetition or other devices.
   2. Sing or play the soprano and bass together. Compare the rhythm and direction of both lines. Name the intervals that are formed by the outer parts.
   3. Sing or play the chorale in four parts. How do the inner parts function melodically and rhythmically? Write out the rhythmic pattern produced by the four voices.

B. Analyze the harmony.
   1. Name the root and quality of each chord.
   2. Discuss the root relationships (circle of fifths, down a third, up a step, etc.).
   3. Identify the cadences. Compare them.
   4. Where do modulations occur? Locate the point at which the movement to the new tonal level seems to begin.
   5. Indicate the harmonic progressions using Roman numerals and figured bass symbols.
   6. How are inversions used?
   7. Circle and name all nonharmonic tones.
   8. How are 7th chords used (preparation, resolution, harmonic functions, etc.)?
   9. How is chromaticism used?
      a. Embellishing chords
      b. Modulation
      c. Color (altered chords)
      d. Stylistic (Picardy third)

C. What are the contributing features to the over-all rhythmic flow in the chorale?
   1. Nonharmonic tones
   2. Rate of chord change
   3. Harmonic tensions and relaxations

A. Bach, *Nun danket alle Gott*
   Rhythm and intervals:

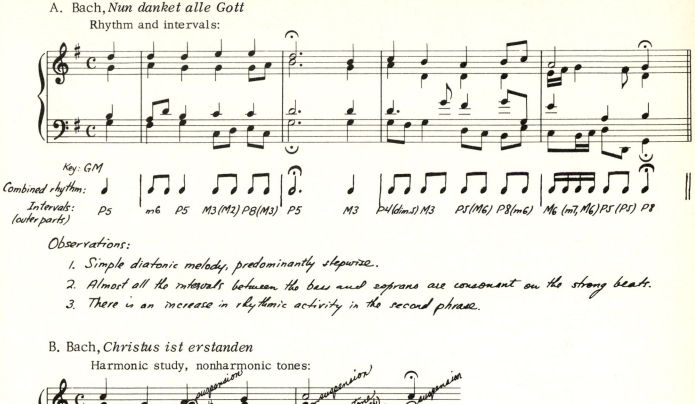

Key: GM

Combined rhythm:

Intervals: P5   m6   P5   M3(M2) P8(M3) P5   M3 P4(dim.5) M3 P5(M6) P8(m6) M6 (m7, M6) P5 (P5) P8
(outer parts)

Observations:

1. *Simple diatonic melody, predominantly stepwise.*

2. *Almost all the intervals between the bass and soprano are consonant on the strong beats.*

3. *There is an increase in rhythmic activity in the second phrase.*

B. Bach, *Christus ist erstanden*
   Harmonic study, nonharmonic tones:

Key: CM

Root:	C	G	F#	G	C	F	C
Chord quality :	M	M	dim.	M	M	M	M
Harmonic function:	I	V₆	VII₆ of V	(dom. 7th) V	(dom. 7th) I₆	IV	I
					V₆ of IV	plagal cadence	

C. Bach, *Freu' dich sehr, o meine Seele*
   Harmonic study, modulation:

GM: I   V₆   ⌈IV₆
   em: ⌊VI₆   V₆   I   IV₆   I₆   V   I

1. Crüger, *Herr, ich habe missgehandelt*

2. Nicolai, *Wachet auf, ruft uns die Stimme*

3. Schop, *Werde munter mein Gemüte*

4. Bach, *Du Friedensfürst, Herr Jesu Christ*

5. Bach, *Nun danket alle Gott*

6. Bach, *Wer weiss, wie nahe mir*

7. Bach, *Werde munter mein Gemüte*

Compare with Chorale No. 3.

8. Bach, *Ermuntre dich, mein schwacher Geist*

9. Bach, *Herr Gott, dich loben alle wir*

10. Bach, *Christus, der ist mein Leben*

11. Bach, *O Haupt voll Blut und Wunden*

12. Bach, *Wachet auf, ruft uns die Stimme*

Compare with Chorale No.2.

13. Bach, *Ach wie nichtig, ach wie flüchtig*

14. Bach, *Jesus, meine Zuversicht*

15. Bach, *Vater unser im Himmelreich*

16. Bach, *Christ lag in Todesbanden*

17. Bach, *Freu' dich sehr, o meine Seele*

Write this chorale using treble and bass clefs.

18. Schumann, *Freue dich, o meine Seele* from *Album für die Jugend,* Op. 68

Compare with Chorale No. 17.

19. Mendelssohn, *Wachet auf, ruft uns die Stimme*

Compare with Chorale No. 2 and No. 12.

20. Persichetti, *Opening Response* from *Hymns and Responses for the Church Year*

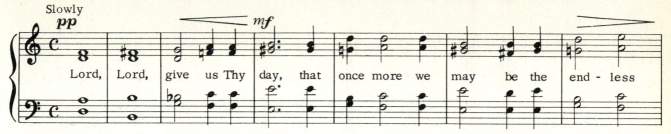

Lord, Lord, give us Thy day, that once more we may be the end - less

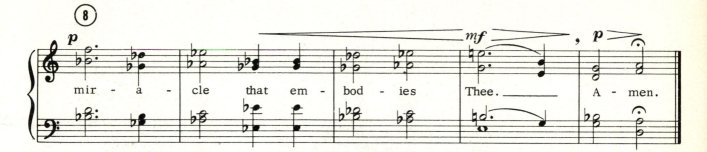

mir - a - cle that em - bod - ies Thee._____ A - men.

UNIT IV

SONGS

SUGGESTIONS AND QUESTIONS FOR ANALYSIS AND DISCUSSION

A. Determine the key.
    1. How is the key established?
    2. What is the key structure?

B. Analyze the vocal line.
    1. Mark the phrase structure.
    2. Point out recurring rhythmic and melodic figures.
    3. Locate the high points.
    4. Indicate other points of interest.

C. Analyze the harmony.
    1. Indicate the harmonic progression using Roman numerals and figured bass symbols.
    2. Circle and name the nonharmonic tones.
    3. Analyze the techniques of modulation.
    4. Study the harmonic rhythm.

D. Examine the texture.
    1. Study the accompaniment patterns.
    2. Are there melodic and contrapuntal elements in the piano part?

E. Discuss those elements that contribute to the structural unity of the work.

F. Study the text.
    1. How is the general mood of the text expressed in the music (accompaniment, change of texture, rhythm, etc.)?
    2. How are important words or phrases highlighted (harmonic change, dynamics, etc.)?

G. Outline the formal structure. To what extent is the form of the piece generated by the text?

Note: English translations of the German words to the songs in Unit IV will be found at the end of the Unit (pages 119-121).

1.

Andante

Haydn

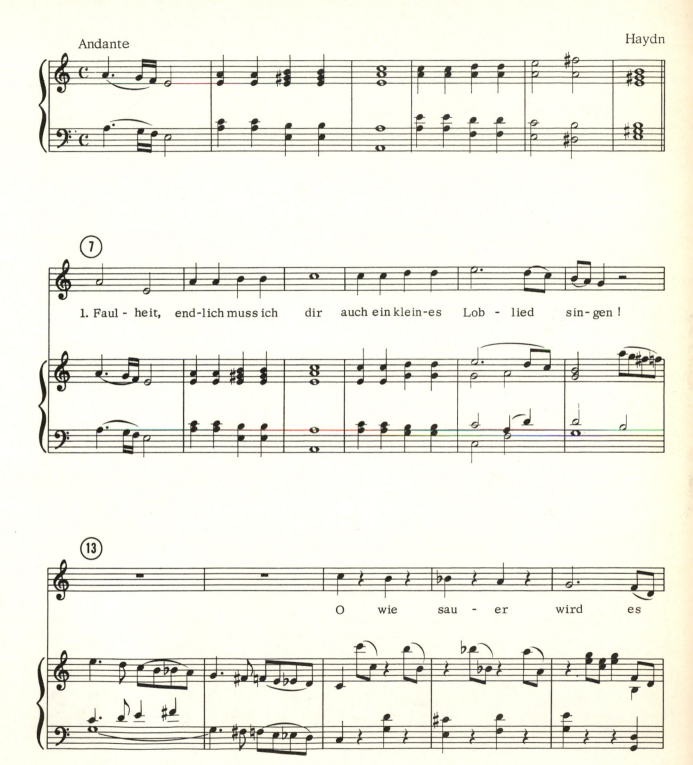

1. Faul - heit, end-lich muss ich dir auch ein klein-es Lob - lied sin-gen!

O wie sau - er wird es

mir, dich nach Würden, dich nach Wür-den zu be-

sin - gen! Doch ich will mein Best - es tun:

nach der Ar - beit ist gut ruh'n.

2.

MORGENGRUSS

from *Die Schöne Müllerin*

Schubert
Op. 25, No. 8

Mässig

1. Gu - ten Mor - gen, schö - ne Mül - le - rin! wo steckst du gleich das
2. O lass mich nur von fer - ne stehn nach dei - nem lie - ben

Köpf - chen hin, als wär dir was ge - sche - hen?
Fen - ster sehn von fer - ne, ganz von fer - ne!

Ver - driesst dich denn mein Gruss so schwer? ver -
Du blon - des Köpf - chen, komm her-vor! her -

stört dich denn mein Blick so sehr? So muss ich wie - der
vor aus eu - rem run - den Tor, ihr blau - en Mor - gen-

ge - hen, so muss ich wie - der ge - hen, wie - der
ster - ne ihr blau - en Mor - gen-ster - ne, ihr Mor - gen-

ge - hen.
ster - ne!

3.

DER MÜLLER UND DER BACH

from *Die Schöne Müllerin*

Schubert
Op. 25, No. 19

Mässig

(Der Müller)

Wo ein treu-es Her - ze in Lie - be ver-

geht, da wel - ken die Li - lien auf je - dem Beet; da muss in die

12 Wol-ken der Voll-mond gehn, da-mit sei-ne Trä-nen die Men-schen nicht

18 sehn; _____ da hal-ten die Eng-lein die Au-gen sich zu und

24 schluch-zen und sin-gen die See-le zur Ruh! Und

(Der Bach)

94

wenn sich die Lie - be dem Schmerz ent - ringt, ein Stern - lein, ein

neu - es, am Him - mel er - blinkt, ein Stern - lein, ein neu - es am

Him - mel er - blinkt; da sprin - gen drei Ro - sen, halb rot und halb

weiss, ___ die wel -ken nicht wie -der, aus Dor - nen - reis; ___ und die

En - ge -lein schnei -den die Flü - gel sich ab und gehn al - le

Mor -gen zur Er - de her - ab, und gehn al - le Mor - gen zur

Er - de her-ab. Ach Bäch - lein, lie-bes Bäch -lein, du

meinst es so gut; ach Bäch - lein, a-ber weisst du, wie Lie - be

tut?_____ Ach un - ten, da un - ten die küh - le

Ruh!___ ach Bäch - lein, lie - bes Bäch - lein, so sin - ge nur zu. ach

Bäch - lein, lie - bes Bäch - lein, so sin - ge nur zu.

4

MIT DEM GRÜNEN LAUTENBANDE

from *Die Schöne Müllerin*

Schubert
Op. 25, No. 13

Mässig

1."Schad um das schö-ne
2. Ist auch dein gan-zer
3. Nun schlin-ge in die

grü-ne Band, dass es ver-bleicht hier an der Wand, ich hab das Grün so
Lieb-ster weiss, soll Grün doch ha-ben sei-nen Preis, und ich auch hab es
Locken dein das grüne Band ge-fäl-lig ein, du hast ja's Grün so

gern, ich hab das Grün so gern!" So sprachst du, Lieb-chen, heut zu mir; gleich
gern, und ich auch hab es gern. Weil uns-re Lieb ist im-mer grün, weil
gern, du hast ja's Grün so gern. Dann weiss ich, wo die Hoffnung wohnt, dann

knüpf ich's ab und send es dir: Nun hab das Grü - ne gern,____ nun
grün der Hoff-nung Fer-nen blühn, drum ha - ben wir es gern,____ drum
weiss ich, wo die Lie-be thront, dann hab ich's Grün erst gern,____ dann

hab das Grü - ne gern!
ha - ben wir es gern.   fine
hab ich's Grün erst gern.

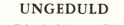

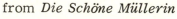

5.

UNGEDULD

from *Die Schöne Müllerin*

Schubert
Op. 25, No. 7

Etwas geschwind

100

1. Ich schnitt' es gern in al - le
2. Ich möcht mir zie - hen ei - nen

Rin - den ein, Ich grüb es gern in je - den Kie - sel - stein, ich
jun - gen Star, bis dass er spräch die Wor - te rein und klar, bis

möcht es sän auf je - des fri - sche Beet mit Kres - sen - sa - men, der es
er sie spräch mit mei - nes Mun - des Klang, mit mei - nes Her - zens vol - lem,

schnell ver - rät, auf je - den wei - ssen Zet - tel möcht ich's schrei - ben:
hei - ssen Drang; dann säng er hell durch ih - re Fen - ster - schei - ben:

Dein ist mein Herz, dein ist mein

Herz und soll es e - wig, e - wig

blei - ben! - ben!

6.

DIE KRÄHE
from *Die Winterreise*

Schubert
Op. 89, No. 15

Etwas langsam

Ei - ne Krä - he

war mit mir aus der Stadt ge - zo - gen,

ist bis heu - te für und für um mein Haupt ge -

flo - gen.

Krä - he, wun - der - li-ches Tier, willst mich nicht ver -

104

las - sen? Meinst wohl bald als Beu - te hier

cresc.

mei - nen Leib zu fas - sen?

Nun, es wird nicht weit mehr gehn an dem Wan - der -

sta - be. Krä - he, lass mich end - lich sehn

cresc.

Treu - e bis zum Gra - be,

f *fz*

Krä - he, lass mich end - lich sehn Treu - e bis zum

p

Gra - be!

7. DU BIST DIE RUH

Schubert
Op. 59, No. 3

Langsàm

Du bist die Ruh, der Frie - de

mild, die Sehn - sucht du, und was sie stillt.

Ich wei - he dir_____ voll Lust und Schmerz zur Woh - nung

hier _____ mein Aug und Herz, _____ mein Aug und Herz. _____

pp

Kehr ein bei mir, und schlie - sse du still hin - ter

dir die Pfor - ten zu. Treib an - dern Schmerz___

aus die - ser Brust! voll sei dies Herz ___ von dei - ner

Lust, ___ von dei - ner Lust. ___

Dies Au - gen - zelt, von

dei - nem Glanz al - lein er - hellt,_____

cresc.

f

o füll es ganz, ____ o füll es ganz! ____

pp

Dies Au - gen - zelt, von dei - nem Glanz al -

cresc.

lein er - hellt, _____ o füll es ganz, _____

pp

f

pp

o füll es ganz! _____

8.

DIE LOTOSBLUME

from *Myrthen*

Schumann
Op. 25, No. 7

Ziemlich langsam

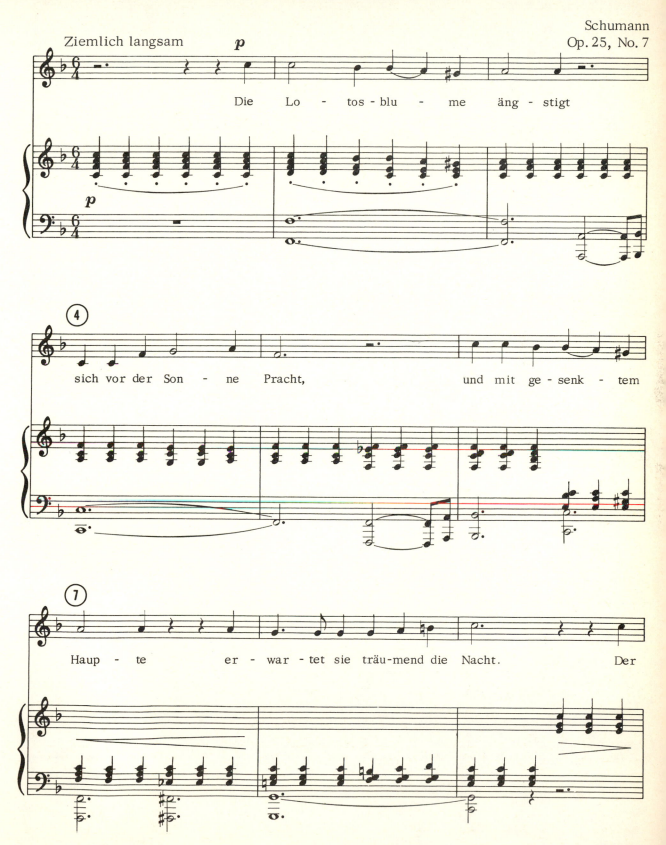

Die Lo - tos - blu - me äng - stigt

sich vor der Son - ne Pracht, und mit ge - senk - tem

Haup - te er - war - tet sie träu - mend die Nacht. Der

Mond, der ist___ ihr Buh - le, er weckt sie mit sei - nem

Licht, und ihm ent-schlei-ert sie freund - lich ihr

poco a poco accel. - -

from - mes Blu - men-ge - sicht. Sie blüht und glüht und

114

leuch - tet, und star - ret stumm in die Höh', _____ sie

rit. **p**

duf - tet und wei - net und zit - tert vor Lie - be und Lie - bes -

rit. - - - - -

weh, vor Lie - be und Lie - bes - weh.

9

DAS VERLASSENE MÄGDLEIN

Wolf

Früh, wann die Häh-ne krähn,

eh die Stern-lein schwin-den, muss ich am Her-de stehn, muss Feu-er

zün-den. Schön ist der Flam-men Schein,

es springen die Fun - ken; ich schau - e so dar-ein, in Lied ver-

sun - ken.

Plötz-lich, da kommt es mir, treu - lo - ser Kna - be,

31 *etwas ruhiger*

dass ich die Nacht von dir ge - trau - met ha - be.

36 *wie zu Anfang*

Trä - ne auf Trä - ne dann stür - zet her -

41

nie - der; so kommt der Tag her-an o ging er

46

wie-der!

Praise to Idleness

(Lob der Faulheit)

Idleness, finally I must sing a little praise-song to you too!
O! how difficult it is for me to sing your praises with dignity!
But I will do my best:
After work it is good to rest.

Morning Greeting

(Morgengruss)

1. Good morning, lovely millermaid!
   Why do you hide your head as if something would happen to you?
   Does my greeting trouble you so?
   Does my look disturb you so?
   Then I must be gone.

2. O let me stay only in the distance,
   And at your dear window gaze from afar, from very far.
   Fair head, come out!
   Open you round doors, you blue morning stars,
   You morning stars!

The Miller and the Brook

(Der Müller und der Bach)

The Miller:

"When a faithful heart of love dies,
Then the lilies wither in every garden;
Then the full moon must go behind the clouds,
So that the people may not see her tears;
Then the angels keep their eyes closed
And lament and sing the soul to rest."

The Brook:

"And when love escapes from pain,
A star, a new one, shines in heaven;
Then spring up three roses, half red and half white,
They will not wither on the thorny bush;
And the angels cut off their wings
And descend every day to earth."

The Miller:

"O little brook, beloved brook, you mean so well;
O little brook, but do you know what Love does?
O below, there below is cool peace!
O little brook, dearest little brook, keep singing to me."

With the Green Lute-Ribbon

(Mit dem grünen Lautenbande)

1. "It's a pity that the pretty green ribbon should fade here upon
        the wall,
   For I am so fond of green,
   For I am so fond of green!"
   This, my love, you said to me today,
   And so I untie it and send it to you;
   Now may you enjoy the green,
   Now may you enjoy the green!

2. Although white may be the dearest, yet green has its value,
   And I like it too,
   And I like it too.
   Because our love is always green,
   Because the far distances of hope are green,
   That is why we are so fond of it,
   That is why we are so fond of it.

3. Now twine the pleasing green ribbon in your hair,
   Since you love green so.
   Since you love green so.
   Then I shall know where hope dwells,
   Then I shall know where love is enthroned,
   And I shall love green first of all,
   And I shall love green first of all.

Impatience

(Ungeduld)

1. I would like to carve it on every tree,
   I would like to engrave it on every stone,
   I wish to sow it in each new garden bed
   In cress seeds which would quickly sprout,
   On every white scrap I wish to write:
   "Thine is my heart, thine is my heart and will be thine forever!"

2. I would teach a young starling
   Till it spoke the words cleanly and clearly,
   Till it spoke them with the sound of my own voice,
   With the ardent longing of my own full heart;
   It would then sing clearly at her window:
   "Thine is my heart, thine is my heart and will be thine forever!"

The Raven

(Die Krähe)

A raven has come with me all the way from town
And today, still flies round and round my head.
"Raven, strange creature, won't you ever leave me?
Do you intend to seize my corpse, soon, as your prey?"
Now I cannot go much further with my walking stick.
"Raven, let me finally see faithfulness unto the grave."

You Are Rest

(Du bist die Ruh)

You are rest, mild peace;
You are desire, and stillness.
I give to you my eyes and heart,
Full of joy and pain, as a dwelling here.
Enter into me and close the gate quietly.
Drive out other pain from this breast!
Filled be this heart with your joy, with your joy.
Your glance alone brightens this enclosure.
O fill it all, O fill it all!

The Lotus-Flower

(Die Lotosblume)

The lotus-flower is afraid of the sun's splendor,
And with sunken head she waits dreamily for the night.
The moon is her lover,
He awakens her with his light,
And to him she unfolds her artless flower-face.
She blooms and glows and shines,
And gazes quietly on high;
She pants and weeps, and trembles
For love and love's pain, for love and love's pain.

The Forsaken Maiden

(Das verlassene Mägdlein)

Early, when the cocks crow,
Before the little stars fade out,
I must stand at the hearth,
And I must light a fire.
The glow of the flames is beautiful,
The sparks fly.
I look into it deep in sorrow.
Suddenly it comes to me, faithless boy,
That I have dreamt of you during the night.
Tears after tears fall down,
And so the day appears.
Oh, I wish it would end.

EXAMPLES OF FIGURED BASS

SUGGESTIONS AND QUESTIONS FOR ANALYSIS AND DISCUSSION

A. Perform the music without realizing the figured bass symbols.
    1. Discuss the relationship between the parts.

B. What is the significance of the figured bass symbols?

C. Realize the figured bass using block chords.

D. Analyze the work.
    1. Harmony
    2. Use of themes
    3. Form
    4. Texture

E. Invent an accompaniment pattern using the given figured bass.

F. Write a new solo part (for violin, flute, or voice) in place of one of the upper parts. Perform it with the continuo part.

G. Look up other examples of figured bass. Realize the figures.

1.

TRIO SONATA IN F MAJOR
(First Movement)

Corelli

FLUTE SONATA IN B MINOR
(First Movement)

Handel

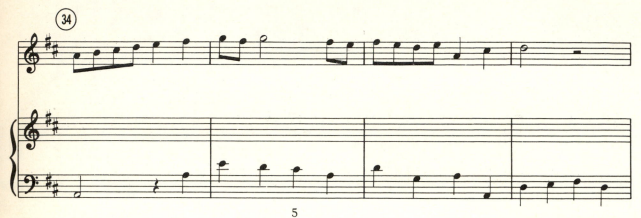

RECITATIVE

from *Cantata 140, Wachet auf*

Bach

UNIT VI

THE LARGER FORMS

SUGGESTIONS AND QUESTIONS FOR ANALYSIS AND DISCUSSION

A. Prepare a melodic analysis of the work.
1. Phrase grouping
2. Melodic design
3. Rhythmic features
4. Harmonic implications
5. High points

B. Outline the formal structure.
1. Key relationships
2. Grouping into large sections
3. Connecting material
4. Climax
5. Comparative study of recurring sections
6. Balance and proportion

C. Analyze the harmonic organization.
1. Chord functions
2. Modulations
3. Harmonic rhythm
4. Texture and accompaniments
5. Specific chords used dramatically

D. Point out the developmental features.
1. Use of motives
2. Compositional devices
3. Use of keys as an element of development
4. Extension or contraction of related ideas
5. Metric and rhythmic shifts
6. Development of textures
7. Use of dynamics
8. Tension and relaxation
9. Use of contrast

E. Discuss idiomatic writing for the instrument(s).

F. Make a comparative stylistic study of the works.

SONATA IN E MINOR

(First Movement)

Haydn

cres - - cen - - do

2.

SONATA
(First Movement)

Mozart, K. 332

Allegro

138

3.

SONATA
(First Movement)

Beethoven
Op. 10, No. 1

Allegro molto e con brio

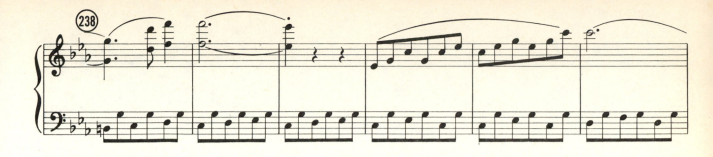

STRING QUARTET
(First Movement)

Allegro vivace assai

164

5.

SONATA
(Second Movement)

Beethoven
Op. 13

Adagio cantabile

171

SONATA

(Third Movement)

Rondo
Allegro commodo

Beethoven
Op. 14, No. 1

UNIT VII

INSTRUMENTAL EXCERPTS

SUGGESTIONS AND QUESTIONS FOR ANALYSIS AND DISCUSSION

A. Discuss the instrumentation.
   1. Arrangement of the symphonic score
   2. Range and characteristics of the individual instruments
   3. Problems of transposing instruments

B. Analyze the score.
   1. Indicate the significant themes.
   2. Using Roman numerals and figured bass symbols, identify the harmonic progressions.
   3. Outline the formal structure.
   4. Discuss the orchestration.

C. Make a transcription of passages from the score for one or two pianos.

D. Transcribe passages from the score for instruments available in class. Perform the transcriptions.

E. How does the orchestra of Wagner differ from that of Haydn?

F. Look up other scores by significant composers. How does the instrumentation compare with that of Haydn?

MINUET
from *Divertimento in B♭*

TRIO

Menuetto da capo

MINUET

from *Symphony No. 53, L'Impériale*

Haydn

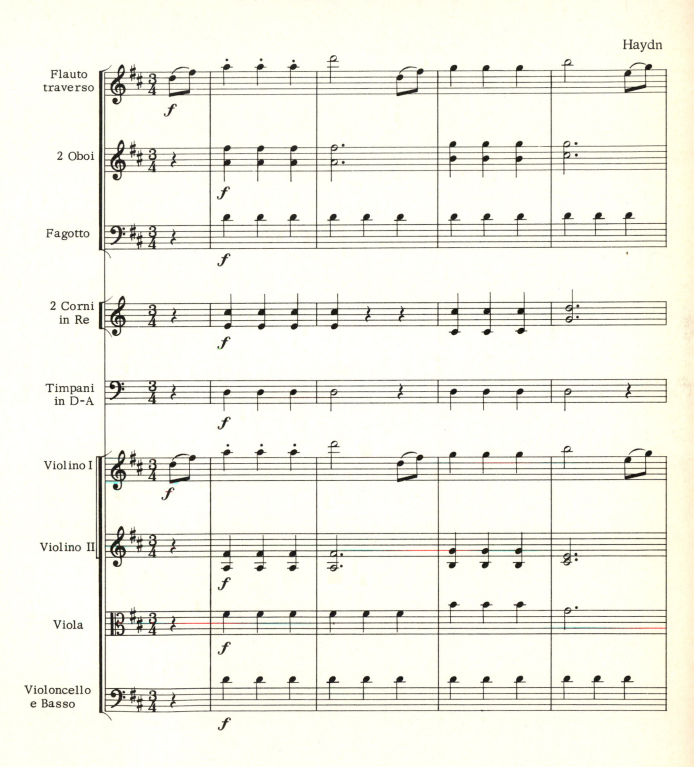

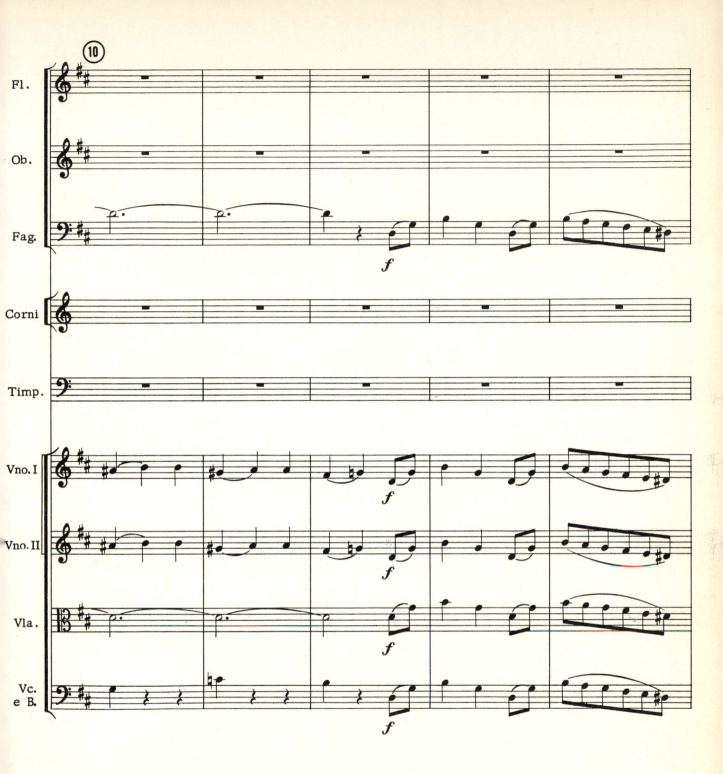

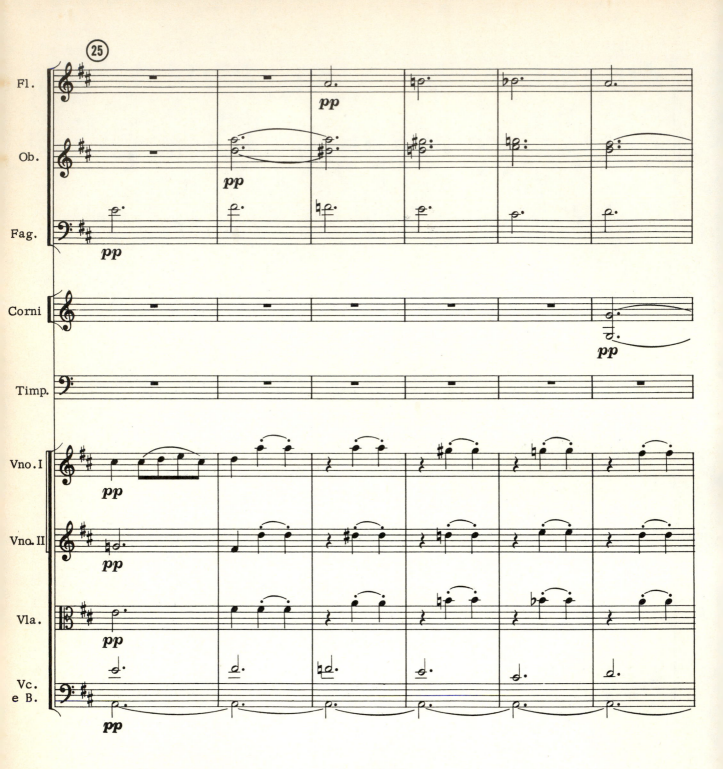

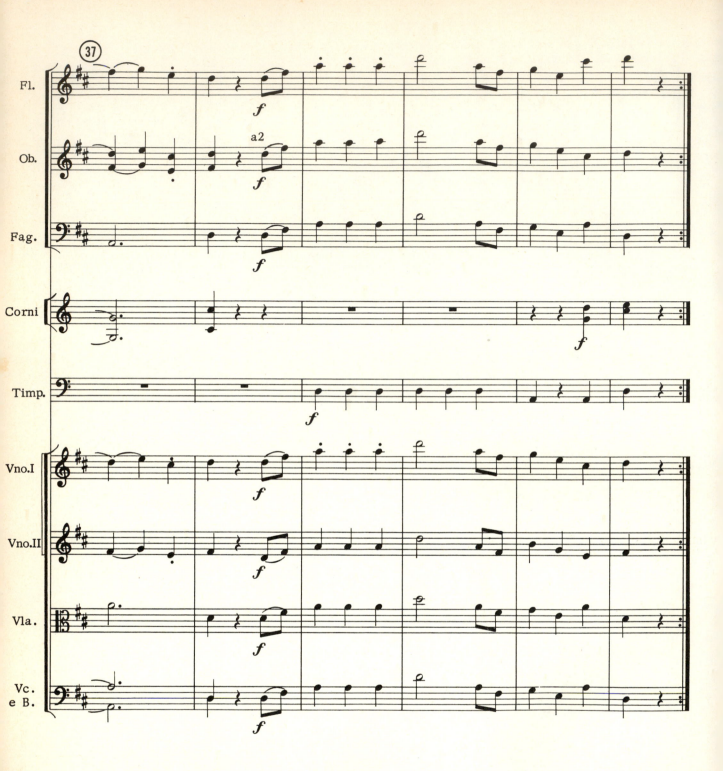

TRIO

Menuetto da capo

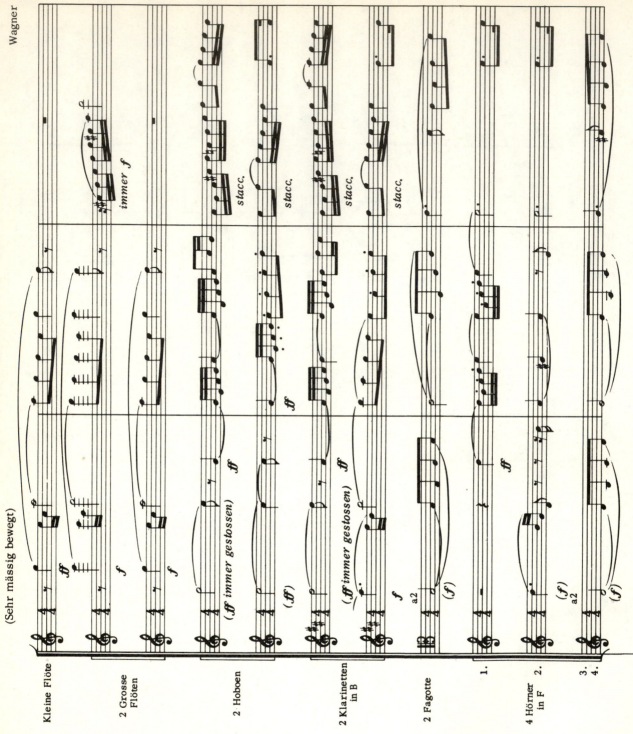

OVERTURE

to *Die Meistersinger von Nürnberg*, Excerpt

Wagner

199

200

201

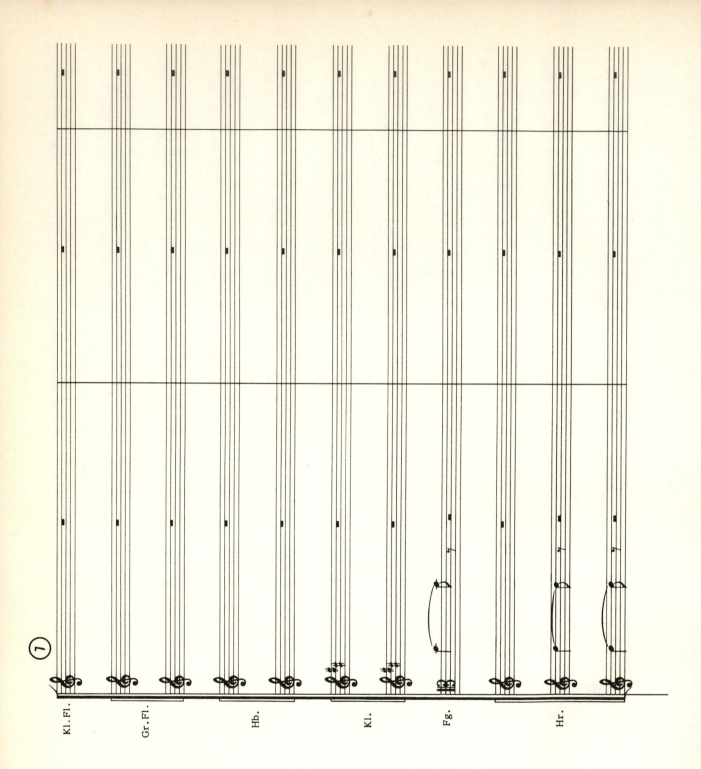

203

APPENDIX

SCALE   An arrangement of pitches in ascending and/or descending order. A scale may be
identified by the number of pitches used and their intervallic relationships. Scales
may include any number of tones (a two-octave scale, for example, may have tones
in the upper octave which differ from those in the lower octave.) Some of the com-
monly used scales are:

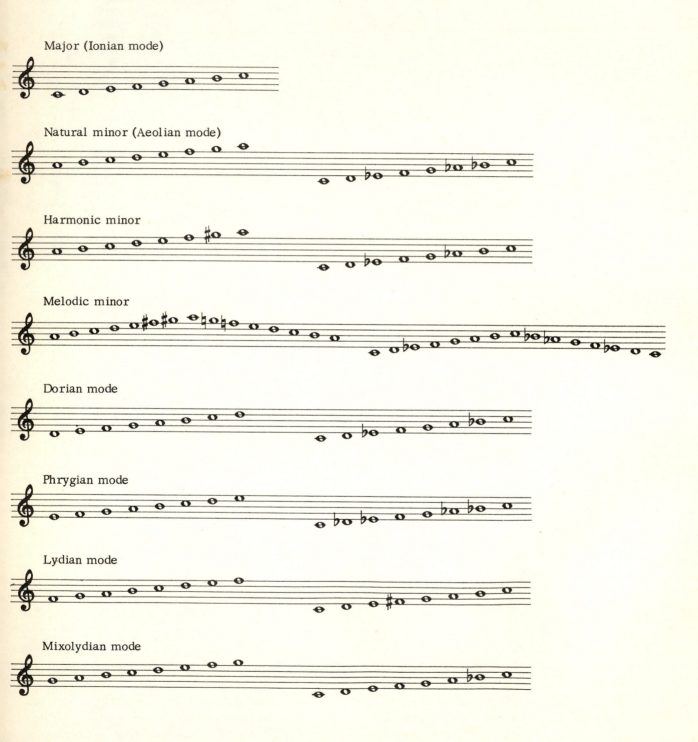

Major (Ionian mode)

Natural minor (Aeolian mode)

Harmonic minor

Melodic minor

Dorian mode

Phrygian mode

Lydian mode

Mixolydian mode

CLEFS

Symbols written on the staff to indicate pitch. Clefs in common use are: G clef (𝄞) indicating G above middle C, F clef (𝄢) indicating F below middle C, and C clef (𝄡) indicating middle C.

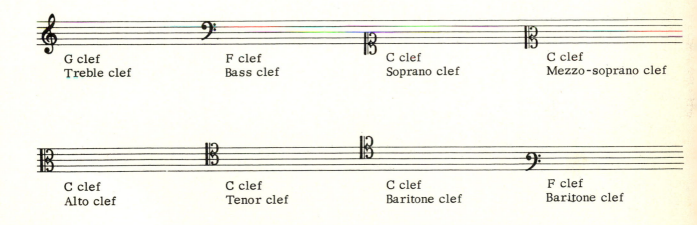

G clef
Treble clef

F clef
Bass clef

C clef
Soprano clef

C clef
Mezzo-soprano clef

C clef
Alto clef

C clef
Tenor clef

C clef
Baritone clef

F clef
Baritone clef

KEY RELATIONSHIP

The degree of affinity between keys. Close relationships are said to exist between a key and its relative major or minor, such as D major and B minor. Other relationships considered close are those keys which are one sharp or one flat key removed from a basic key center (in D major: A major, G major, F♯ minor, E minor.) Keys having the same tonic are called parallel major and parallel minor. All keys stand in some relationship to each other but in varying degrees of relatedness.

COMPOSITIONAL DEVICE

Repetition of a musical idea through which a composer may achieve unity in a composition. Some examples of frequently used compositional devices follow:

Exact repetition

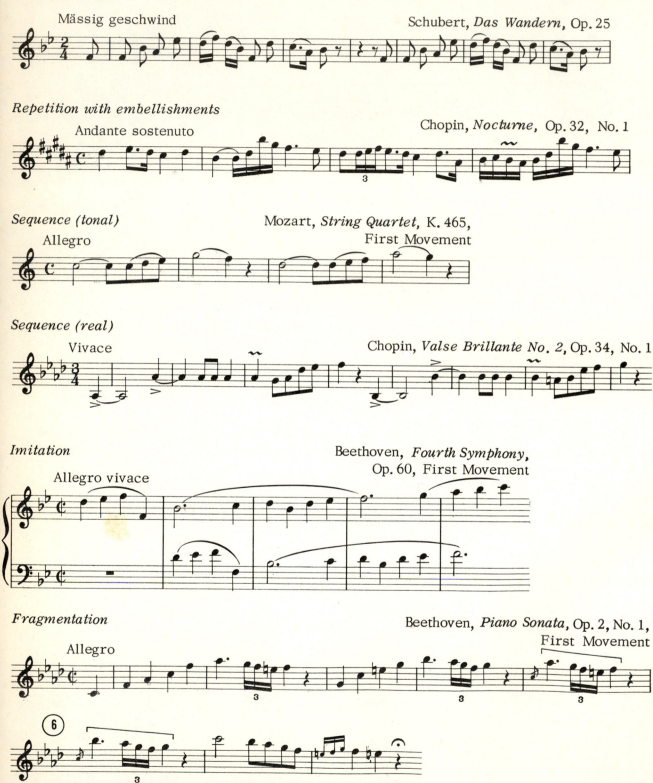

Repetition with embellishments

Sequence (tonal)

Sequence (real)

Imitation

Fragmentation

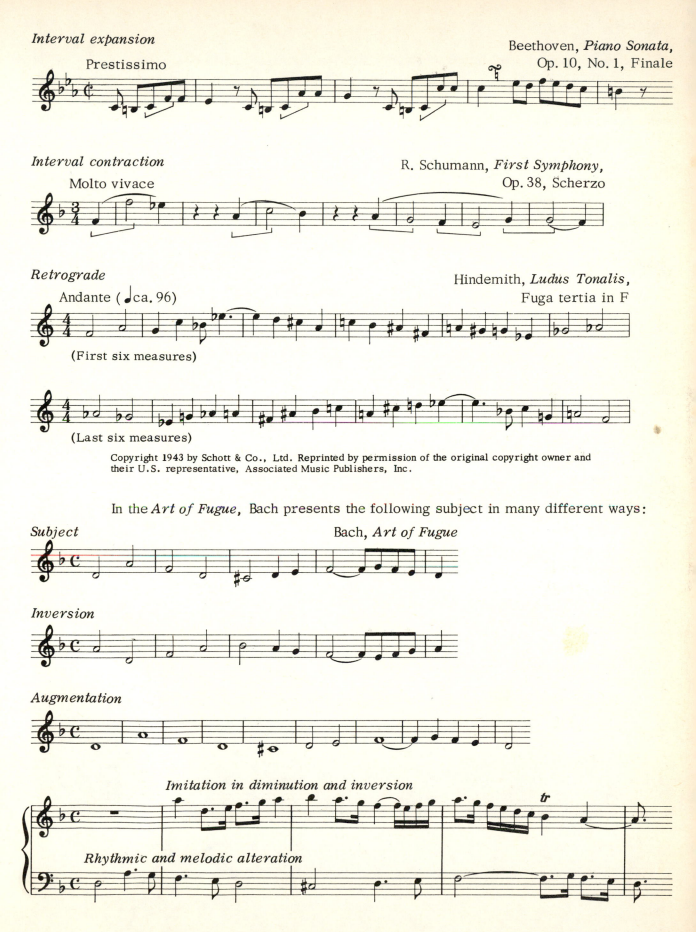

Interval expansion

Prestissimo

Beethoven, *Piano Sonata,* Op. 10, No. 1, Finale

Interval contraction

Molto vivace

R. Schumann, *First Symphony,* Op. 38, Scherzo

Retrograde

Andante (♩ca. 96)

Hindemith, *Ludus Tonalis,* Fuga tertia in F

(First six measures)

(Last six measures)

In the *Art of Fugue,* Bach presents the following subject in many different ways:

Subject

Bach, *Art of Fugue*

Inversion

Augmentation

Imitation in diminution and inversion

Rhythmic and melodic alteration

CADENCE

A melodic or harmonic point of rest. Some characteristic harmonic cadence formulas follow:

Authentic cadence

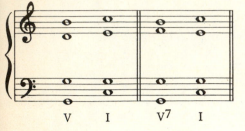

Plagal cadence   *Semi cadence*

Deceptive cadence   *Phrygian cadence*

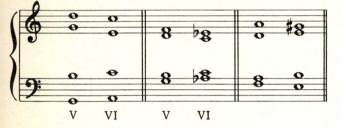

NONHARMONIC TONES (NON-CHORD TONES)

Pitches which are foreign to the prevailing harmony. Some typical examples follow:

Passing tones   *Upper auxiliary*   *Lower auxiliary*   *Changing tones*

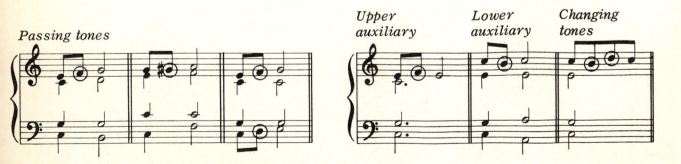

Suspension Appoggiatura Anticipation Escape tone

FORM   A general term used in reference to the design or structure of a musical composition.

Under this broad heading, the following terms are frequently used:

Motive – Short melodic pattern or rhythmic figure which recurs significantly in a composition.

Phrase – A unified musical thought coming to a point of rest.

Period – Usually two or more phrases related by unity of melody, rhythm, tonality, and texture.

Section – A cohesive group of phrases or periods comprising a major subdivision of a work (such as a "development" or "transition" section).

Binary – A form which is divided into two unified parts, usually:

$$\|{:}\quad a\quad {:}\|{:}\quad b\quad {:}\|$$

or $\|{:}\ a\ {:}\|{:}\ b\quad a\ {:}\|$ (Rounded)

Ternary – Two contrasting sections (A and B) followed by a return of the first section (A) (as in a Minuet and Trio movement).

Rondo – A large structure where a principal theme (A) alternates with contrasting material, usually ABACA or ABACABA.

Sonata Allegro – A large structure whose broader outlines are:
1) Exposition
2) Development
3) Recapitulation
The Exposition may be preceded by an Introduction and the Recapitulation may be followed by a Coda.

Theme and Variations – A composition having the principal characteristic of a central musical idea which goes through various transformations.

Numbers written with a bass tone indicating the interval or intervals which should sound with the given bass tone. Figured bass (thorough bass, basso continuo) was used extensively throughout the Baroque Period.

Bass tones acting as the root of a triad frequently have no figure or may have any of the following: $\frac{8}{5}$, $\frac{5}{3}$, $\frac{8}{5}$, $\frac{8}{3}$, 5, 3.

Symbols indicating a triad in first inversion may be: 6, $\frac{6}{3}$, $\frac{8}{6}$.

Symbols indicating a triad in second inversion may be: $\frac{6}{4}$, $\frac{8}{6}$.

Symbols indicating a 7th chord in root position may be: 7, $\frac{7}{3}$, $\frac{7}{5}$, $\frac{7}{5}$.

Symbols indicating a 7th chord in first inversion may be: $\frac{6}{5}$, $\frac{6}{5}$.

Symbols indicating a 7th chord in second inversion may be: $\frac{4}{3}$, $\frac{6}{4}$.

Symbols indicating a 7th chord in third inversion may be: 2, $\frac{4}{2}$, $\frac{6}{4}$.

A stroke through a number (∅) indicates that that interval will be raised a half step. A flat with a number indicates that that interval will be lowered a half step. An accidental (♮, ♭ or ♯) appearing alone refers to an alteration of the third up from the bass. Other numbers may be used to indicate dissonant tones.

OVERTONES

Higher tones which are present when a fundamental tone is played. These are produced by the vibrations of small sections of a string or air column. Overtones occur in a regular series in which the intervallic distance between the pitches gradually decreases in size and the pitches decrease in intensity. The overtone series up from C is:

Those instruments which sound pitches other than those which are notated. To determine the sound that will be produced when a certain note is written, the following formula may be applied: When a "C" is *written*, the *sound* will be that of the key of the instrument. For example: a B♭ clarinet will sound "B♭" when "C" is written. Therefore, the B♭ clarinet will sound a whole step under the written tone (or, conversely, parts for the B♭ clarinet are written a whole step above the desired sounds). Illustrations of other transpositions follow:

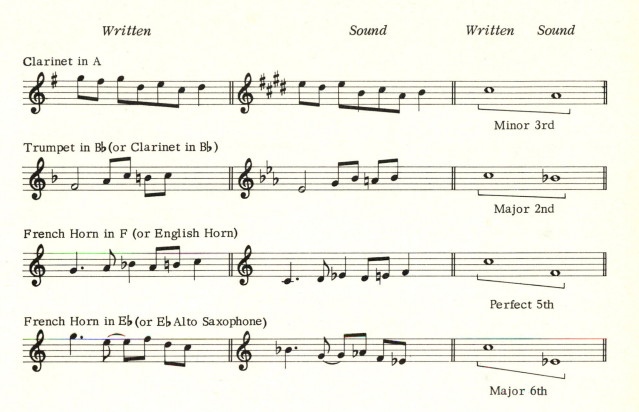

Written   *Sound*   *Written*   *Sound*

Clarinet in A

Minor 3rd

Trumpet in B♭ (or Clarinet in B♭)

Major 2nd

French Horn in F (or English Horn)

Perfect 5th

French Horn in E♭ (or E♭ Alto Saxophone)

Major 6th

Bach (1685-1750)
Bartók (1881-1945)
Beethoven (1770-1827)
Brahms (1833-1897)
Byrd (1543-1623)
Chopin (1810-1849)
Copland (1900-   )
Corelli (1653-1713)
Crüger (1598-1662)
Debussy (1862-1918)
Fauré (1845-1924)
Handel (1685-1759)
Harris (1898-   )
Haydn (1732-1809)
Hindemith (1895-   )
Machaut (c.1300-1377)
Mendelssohn (1809-1847)
Milhaud (1892-   )
Moussorgsky (1839-1881)

Mozart (1756-1791)
Nicolai (1556-1608)
Palestrina (c.1524-1594)
Persichetti (1915-   )
Prokofieff (1891-1953)
Purcell (1658-1695)
Rameau (1683-1764)
Schönberg (1874-1951)
Schop (-c. 1664)
Schubert (1797-1828)
Schuman, (1910-   )
Schumann, (1810-1856)
Schütz (1585-1672)
Strauss (1864-1949)
Stravinsky (1882-   )
Tchaikovsky (1840-1893)
Vivaldi (c.1676-1741)
Wagner (1813-1883)
Wolf (1860-1903)

Printer and Binder: The Murray Printing Company

80 9 8